Greater Than Us All

PHOTOGRAPHY BY MARK MABRY AND SCOTT SUMNER

Library of Congress Cataloging-in-Publication Data
Cope, Kenneth, author.
    Greater Than Us All / Kenneth Cope.
        pages cm
    Includes bibliographical references.
    Summary: Musical artist Kenneth Cope reflects on the Savior, Jesus Christ.
    ISBN 978-1-60907-319-0 (hardbound w/cd: alk. paper)
    1. Jesus Christ. 2. The Church of Jesus Christ of Latter-day Saints—Doctrines. 3. Mormon Church—Doctrines. I. Title.
    BX8643.J4C67 2013
    232—dc23
                                                                                    2012043322

Printed in China
Four Colour Print Group
10   9   8   7   6   5   4   3   2   1

Greater Than Us All

KENNETH COPE

DESERET
BOOK

SALT LAKE CITY, UTAH

Before we all came to earth
We lived together with
God in His world

For I, the Lord God, *created all things*, of which I have spoken, spiritually, before they were naturally upon the face of the earth. . . . And I, the Lord God, had created all the children of men; and not yet a man to till the ground; for in heaven created I them.

—Moses 3:5

Man was also in the beginning with God.

—Doctrine and Covenants 93:29

He helped His children progress

Yet one advanced so much more than the rest

Firstborn

*T*he spirits of men, while yet in the Eternal Presence, developed aptitudes, talents, capacities, and abilities of every sort, kind, and degree.... As the ages rolled, no two spirits remained alike.... Some excelled in one way, others in another. *The Firstborn excelled all of us in all things.*

—BRUCE R. McCONKIE

He was greater than us all

And there stood one among them that was like unto God. . . . And the Lord said: Whom shall I send? And one answered like unto the Son of Man: *Here am I, send me.*

—ABRAHAM 3:24, 27

Son of Man

Then father offered a plan

We are the spirit offspring of a loving God, our Heavenly Father. He has a great plan of salvation whereby His children might be perfected as He is and might have a *fulness of joy* as He enjoys.

—Ezra Taft Benson

God so loved the world, that he gave his only begotten Son, that whosoever believeth in him should not perish, but have *everlasting life.*

—John 3:16

He'd send us off with a way to return again

*I*n our premortal state we shouted for joy as the plan of salvation was unfolded to our view. It was there our elder brother Jesus, the firstborn in the spirit of our Father's children, volunteered to redeem us from our sins. He became our foreordained *Savior,* the Lamb "slain from the foundation of the world" (Moses 7:47).

—EZRA TAFT BENSON

of the World

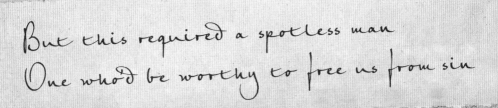

But this required a spotless man
One who'd be worthy to free us from sin

As we think about Christ's life, we are amazed
in every way. . . . Jesus Christ was the purest and only
perfect person who ever lived.

—JEFFREY R. HOLLAND

Someone, greater than us all

$\mathcal{T}$he offer of the firstborn Son to establish through His own ministry among men the gospel of salvation, and to *sacrifice Himself,* through labor, humiliation and suffering even unto death, was accepted and made the foreordained plan of man's redemption from death, of his eventual salvation from the effects of sin, and of his possible exaltation.

—JAMES E. TALMAGE

Lamb of God

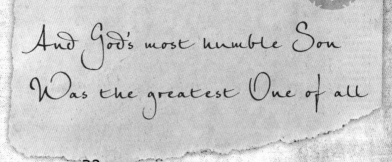

And God's most humble Son
Was the greatest One of all

God, the Father, gave His Son, and Jesus Christ gave us the Atonement, the *greatest of all gifts* and all giving. . . . Jesus gave the gift freely, willingly, to us all. He said, "Therefore doth my Father love me, because I lay down my life, that I might take it again. No man taketh it from me, but I lay it down of myself" (John 10:17-18). All men and women come into this life with that gift. They will live again, and if they will, they may live with Him.

—HENRY B. EYRING

Mediator

We looked on Him

God's best son

As the only *Perfect Person* to sojourn on this planet, there is none like Him! In intelligence and performance, He far surpasses the individual and the composite capacities and achievements of all who have lived, live now, and will yet live!

—NEAL A. MAXWELL

*Would He give His great life for us
Pay the price for all our sins*

From the time of the premortal council, in which Jesus became the Christ, the Messiah, the *Savior of all mankind,* through his millennial reign, he has and will persevere in perfection, doing all that his Father commanded. Because of his love for us, he offered to fulfill the plan of salvation with these words, "Father, thy will be done, and the glory be thine forever" (Moses 4:2).

—JOSEPH B. WIRTHLIN

Messiah

*And knowing no other could
He humbly said He would*

Christ our Lord, Firstborn of the Father, mightiest of all the spirit host, a Man like unto his Father. . . . Before he took upon himself flesh and blood he was the Great Jehovah, the Eternal One, [the] Great I AM. He stood next to the Father, and became . . . the Creator of *all things* from the beginning. . . . When such a life is projected from its eternal home into our mortal sphere, can anyone suppose that it could be other than the greatest life ever lived?

—Bruce R. McConkie

The Great I Am

He was greater than us all
God's most humble Son was the greatest one

*O*nly when we understand the ministry of Jesus Christ, in which he also had a preeminence in the premortal world, do we begin to get some sense of the sweep of the Savior's labors for and *in behalf* of all of us.

—Spencer W. Kimball

Every heart felt of His love
for us He'd come
The greatest one of all

The magnificent expression of His love came in His death when He gave His life as a sacrifice for all men. . . . No other act in all of human history compares with it. Nothing that has ever happened can match it. Totally unselfish and with unbounded love for all mankind, it became an unparalleled act of mercy for the whole human race.

—GORDON B. HINCKLEY

We love him, because he first loved us.

—1 JOHN 4:19

Beloved

About the Author

"I decided a long time ago that I was going to devote my energy and my talents to making the name of Jesus Christ greater on the earth," Kenneth says. "And that is what I am about. It propels every choice, every decision. I hope to create new ways for people to see Jesus Christ—to offer a new vantage point and open eyes, to show how He is in everything. I am passionate about Him, and I want that passion to flow out of everything I do."

Motivated by such passion, few musicians have impacted a culture or genre as acutely and intensely as has this composer, producer, performer, songwriter, and singer. He consistently sets the standard for excellence in inspirational LDS music.

Kenneth was born in Salt Lake City, the third of six children. He grew up mostly in Houston, Texas, where he attended the High School for the Performing and Visual Arts. He later served an LDS mission to Switzerland and France. He began his singing/songwriting career by recording the 1986 Especially for Youth (EFY) theme song and has gone on to compose more than twenty-five songs for the EFY Program.

Some of Kenneth's songs like "His Hands" and "Never a Better Hero" have become Latter-day Saint classics. Kenneth has produced eleven albums of his own and has created a two-act musical for the stage about the life of Christ titled *Son of Man*.

Photo by Russ Dixon

"I strongly believe that if we are doing with our lives those things God wants us to do, He will open the way for us to continue in our path and consistently bring about more good," Kenneth says.

Recognizing Kenneth's achievements, the Faith Centered Music Association (FCMA) has awarded him numerous PEARL Awards over the years, including Male Vocalist of the Year, Songwriter of the Year, and Album of the Year.

Kenneth lives with his wife, Kathy, and their three daughters in Salt Lake City, Utah.

Sources

p. 3: Bruce R. McConkie, *The Mortal Messiah* (Salt Lake City: Deseret Book Co., 1981), vol. 1, 23.

p. 7: Ezra Taft Benson, in *The Prophets Have Spoken*, comp. Eric D. Bateman, 3 vols. (Salt Lake City: Deseret Book, 1999), 3:1068.

p. 9: Ezra Taft Benson, "He Lives," *New Era*, April 1986, 4.

p. 11: Jeffrey R. Holland, "Amazed at the Love Jesus Offers Me," *New Era*, December 2008, 3–4.

p. 12: James E. Talmage, *Jesus the Christ* (Salt Lake City: Deseret Book, 1949), 18.

p. 15: Henry B. Eyring, *Because He First Loved Us* (Salt Lake City: Deseret Book, 2002), 220–21.

p. 16: Neal A. Maxwell, "'O, Divine Redeemer,'" *Ensign*, November 1981, 80.

p. 19: Joseph B. Wirthlin, "Never Give Up," *Ensign*, November 1987, 10.

p. 21: Bruce R. McConkie, *The Mortal Messiah* (Salt Lake City: Deseret Book Co., 1981), vol. 1, 26–27.

p. 23: Spencer W. Kimball, "The Savior: The Center of Our Lives," *New Era*, April 1980, 33.

p. 24: Gordon B. Hinckley, "At the Summit of the Ages," *Ensign*, November 1999, 73.

Image Credits

Page iv: *Stars* © Mark Mabry

Pages 2–3: *By Mine Only Begotten* © Scott Sumner

Page 5: *I Am* © Scott Sumner

Page 6: *Husband* © Mark Mabry

Page 8: *King of Kings* © Scott Sumner

Page 10: *Fount of Living Water* © Scott Sumner

Page 13: *The Comforter* © Scott Sumner

Page 14: *Golgotha* © Scott Sumner

Page 17: *Walking on Water* © Mark Mabry

Page 18: *Tempted in All Things* © Scott Sumner

Page 20: *Light and Life* © Mark Mabry

Pages 22–23: *Remember* © Mark Mabry

Page 25: *One by One* © Scott Sumner

Backgrounds: Shutterstock Images

All photographs and illustrations throughout the book are used by permission.